You a Ewe?

by Rebecca Felix

amicus readers

Ideas for Parents and Teachers

Amicus Readers let children practice reading informational texts at the earliest reading levels. Familiar words and concepts with close photo-text matches support early readers.

Before Reading

- Discuss the cover photo with the child. What does it tell him?
- Ask the child to predict what she will learn in the book.

Read the Book

- "Walk" through the book and look at the photos. Let the child ask questions.
- Read the book to the child, or have the child read independently.

After Reading

- Use the matching quiz at the end of the book to review the text.
- Prompt the child to make connections. Ask: *Can you think of other words that sound the same but have different meanings and spellings?*

Amicus Readers are published by Amicus
P.O. Box 1329, Mankato, MN 56002
www.amicuspublishing.us

Copyright © 2015. International copyright reserved in all countries. No part of this book may be reproduced in any form without written permission from the publisher.

Library of Congress Cataloging-in-Publication Data

Felix, Rebecca, 1984-
  Are you a ewe? / Rebecca Felix.
     pages cm -- (Hear homophones here)
  Audience: K to Grade 3.
  Audience: Age 6
  ISBN 978-1-60753-568-3 (hardcover) --
  ISBN 978-1-60753-652-9 (pdf ebook)
  1. English language--Homonyms--Juvenile literature.
  2. Farms--Juvenile literature. I. Title.
  PE1595.F35 2014
  428.1--dc23

                          2013048619

Photo Credits: Shutterstock Images, cover, 1, 3, 5, 8 (bottom left), 12–13, 16 (bottom left), 16 (bottom right); Jakkrit Panalee/Shutterstock Images, 6; Barry Blackburn/Shutterstock Images, 8–9; Four Oaks/Shutterstock Images, 10, 16 (middle left); Horse Crazy/Shutterstock Images, 11, 16 (top right); Ina van Hateren/Shutterstock Images, 14, 16 (top left); Chronicle Books/José Luis Merino, 16 (middle right)

Produced for Amicus by The Peterson Publishing Company and Red Line Editorial.

Editor Jenna Gleisner
Designer Jake Nordby
Printed in the United States of America
Mankato, MN
2-2014
PA10001
10 9 8 7 6 5 4 3 2 1

Homophones are words that sound the same. But they have different meanings and spellings. What homophones can we find at the farm?

ewe
you

Grace and Eve visit a farm. They see sheep. A **ewe** is a female sheep. "Are **you** a **ewe**?" Grace asks a sheep.

5

hay
hey

A farmer gives the sheep some **hay**. **Hay** is made of dried grasses. "**Hey**, look!" Eve says. "The sheep eat **hay**."

main
mane

Eve and Grace visit the horses next. The horses are in the **main** barn. Each horse's **mane** is long and shiny.

braid
brayed

The girls admired one horse's **braid**. Then they heard a loud sound. A donkey **brayed**. Hee-haw!

herd
heard

A **herd** of cows is in the field. A **herd** is a group. The girls **heard** the **herd** of cows mooing. Moo!

tail
tale

The girls' favorite part is seeing each pig's curly **tail**. They will tell their friends a **tale** about each animal at the farm!

Match each homophone to its picture!

braid

brayed

herd

heard

tail

tale